I0568143

January 1

What hopes do you have for the new year?

_____

_____

_____

_____

_____

_____

_____

_____

_____

_____

_____

_____

_____

January 2

Today, I am feeling...

_____
_____
_____
_____
_____
_____
_____
_____
_____
_____
_____
_____
_____

January 3

What worries are you willing to let go of today?

_____

_____

_____

_____

_____

_____

_____

_____

_____

_____

_____

_____

_____

January 4

With my friend/loved one, what I feel most right now is...

_____

_____

_____

_____

_____

_____

_____

_____

_____

_____

_____

_____

_____

_____

January 5

What made you become a caregiver?

_____

_____

_____

_____

_____

_____

_____

_____

_____

_____

_____

_____

_____

_____

January 6

Do you specialize in what's ailing your friend/loved one?

_____

_____

_____

_____

_____

_____

_____

_____

_____

_____

_____

_____

_____

_____

January 7

What skills make for a great caregiver?

_____

_____

_____

_____

_____

_____

_____

_____

_____

_____

_____

_____

_____

_____

January 8

What makes the biggest difference in your life?

_____
_____
_____
_____
_____
_____
_____
_____
_____
_____
_____
_____
_____

January 9

I wish I was able to better understand...

_____

_____

_____

_____

_____

_____

_____

_____

_____

_____

_____

_____

_____

_____

January 10

To make myself more useful, I could...

_____

_____

_____

_____

_____

_____

_____

_____

_____

_____

_____

_____

_____

January 11

What is a special moment that you have shared with your friend/loved one?

_____

_____

_____

_____

_____

_____

_____

_____

_____

_____

_____

January 12

What is present in your life right now that excites you?

_____

_____

_____

_____

_____

_____

_____

_____

_____

_____

_____

_____

_____

January 13

What brought you joy today?

_____

_____

_____

_____

_____

_____

_____

_____

_____

_____

_____

_____

_____

January 14

How important are career achievements to you?

_____
_____
_____
_____
_____
_____
_____
_____
_____
_____
_____
_____
_____
_____

January 15

If you died today, are you happy with the legacy you'll leave behind?

_____

_____

_____

_____

_____

_____

_____

_____

_____

_____

_____

_____

January 16

How do you feel in this moment?

_____
_____
_____
_____
_____
_____
_____
_____
_____
_____
_____
_____
_____

January 17

How do you handle stress and anxiety effectively?

_____

_____

_____

_____

_____

_____

_____

_____

_____

_____

_____

_____

_____

January 18

How much time do you currently enjoy outside of work or away from your friend/loved one?

_____

_____

_____

_____

_____

_____

_____

_____

_____

_____

_____

_____

_____

January 19

How important is managing routine tasks around the home to you?

_____

_____

_____

_____

_____

_____

_____

_____

_____

_____

_____

_____

_____

January 20

What was the best part of today?

_____
_____
_____
_____
_____
_____
_____
_____
_____
_____
_____
_____

January 21

How do you encourage and support those closest to you?

_____

_____

_____

_____

_____

_____

_____

_____

_____

_____

_____

_____

_____

_____

January 22

How mentally healthy and strong do you currently feel?

_____

_____

_____

_____

_____

_____

_____

_____

_____

_____

_____

_____

_____

_____

January 23

How would other people describe you?

_____

_____

_____

_____

_____

_____

_____

_____

_____

_____

_____

_____

_____

_____

January 24

What are some questions you have asked your friend/loved one?

_____

_____

_____

_____

_____

_____

_____

_____

_____

_____

_____

_____

_____

_____

January 25

Are your current efforts going to help you achieve better life balance? If no, what needs to change?

_____

_____

_____

_____

_____

_____

_____

_____

_____

_____

_____

_____

_____

January 26

Describe your day.

_____

_____

_____

_____

_____

_____

_____

_____

_____

_____

_____

_____

January 27

What are the positives in your life?

_____

_____

_____

_____

_____

_____

_____

_____

_____

_____

_____

_____

_____

January 28

What have you learned about your friend/loved one?

_____

_____

_____

_____

_____

_____

_____

_____

_____

_____

_____

_____

_____

January 29

What would your theme song be for this year?

_____

_____

_____

_____

_____

_____

_____

_____

_____

_____

_____

_____

_____

_____

January 30

How has your friend/loved one had a major impact on your life in the last year? How?

_____

_____

_____

_____

_____

_____

_____

_____

_____

_____

_____

_____

January 31

I practice self-care by _____ .

_____
_____
_____
_____
_____
_____
_____
_____
_____
_____
_____
_____
_____

February 1

What's in your life that is fulfilling and full of potential?

_____

_____

_____

_____

_____

_____

_____

_____

_____

_____

_____

_____

_____

February 2

How might taking better care of yourself help you care for your loved one?

_____

_____

_____

_____

_____

_____

_____

_____

_____

_____

_____

_____

February 3

How do you get what you need without impacting someone else?

_____

_____

_____

_____

_____

_____

_____

_____

_____

_____

_____

_____

February 4

What was the last thing that someone did nice for you?

_____

_____

_____

_____

_____

_____

_____

_____

_____

_____

_____

_____

_____

February 5

Suppose you needed in-home care yourself. What would you look for in a caregiver?

_____

_____

_____

_____

_____

_____

_____

_____

_____

_____

_____

_____

_____

_____

February 6

What activities and commitments have you made that don't suit you?

_____

_____

_____

_____

_____

_____

_____

_____

_____

_____

_____

_____

_____

February 7

How do you avoid burnout?

_____
_____
_____
_____
_____
_____
_____
_____
_____
_____
_____
_____
_____

February 8

With whom are your closest relationships?

_____

_____

_____

_____

_____

_____

_____

_____

_____

_____

_____

_____

_____

_____

February 9

What would you like to remember about your friend/loved one?

_____

_____

_____

_____

_____

_____

_____

_____

_____

_____

_____

_____

February 10

What comforts you?

_____

_____

_____

_____

_____

_____

_____

_____

_____

_____

_____

_____

February 11

What do you need to give up complaining about?

_____
_____
_____
_____
_____
_____
_____
_____
_____
_____
_____
_____
_____
_____

February 12

How important is it for you to check in with your friend/loved one to get a beeter idea of their needs, wants, and desires?

_____

_____

_____

_____

_____

_____

_____

_____

_____

_____

_____

_____

_____

February 13

How comfortable with silence are you?

_____

_____

_____

_____

_____

_____

_____

_____

_____

_____

_____

_____

_____

February 14

How patient are you?

_____

_____

_____

_____

_____

_____

_____

_____

_____

_____

_____

_____

_____

_____

February 15

What issues might your friend/loved one still need to resolve?

_____

_____

_____

_____

_____

_____

_____

_____

_____

_____

_____

_____

February 16

Is there anything that you are currently procrastinating on getting done?

_____

_____

_____

_____

_____

_____

_____

_____

_____

_____

_____

February 17

What can you do in a few minutes each day for self-care?

_____

_____

_____

_____

_____

_____

_____

_____

_____

_____

_____

_____

_____

_____

February 18

Are you a list maker and a planner?

_____
_____
_____
_____
_____
_____
_____
_____
_____
_____
_____
_____
_____
_____

February 19

Do you have a morning routine?

_____
_____
_____
_____
_____
_____
_____
_____
_____
_____
_____
_____
_____
_____

February 20

What travel are you yet to do? Where do you want to go??

_____
_____
_____
_____
_____
_____
_____
_____
_____
_____
_____
_____
_____
_____

February 21

Are there people in your life who are draining your energy and joy?

_____

_____

_____

_____

_____

_____

_____

_____

_____

_____

_____

February 22

Suppose you decided to have your wages paid in something other than money. What would it be and why?

_____

_____

_____

_____

_____

_____

_____

_____

_____

_____

_____

_____

_____

February 23

What are your strengths?

_____

_____

_____

_____

_____

_____

_____

_____

_____

_____

_____

_____

_____

_____

February 24

What can you do for hours on end and often lose track of time?

_____

_____

_____

_____

_____

_____

_____

_____

_____

_____

_____

February 25

How much time do you spend focusing on yourself and your immediate needs?

_____

_____

_____

_____

_____

_____

_____

_____

_____

_____

_____

_____

February 26

What skill are you yet to learn or take up that you've always wanted to?

_____

_____

_____

_____

_____

_____

_____

_____

_____

_____

_____

_____

February 27

Are you able to do things that you enjoy frequently?

_____

_____

_____

_____

_____

_____

_____

_____

_____

_____

_____

_____

_____

February 28

What has been one of the most difficult lessons you've learned as a caregiver?

_____

_____

_____

_____

_____

_____

_____

_____

_____

_____

_____

_____

February 29

Is there a message your friend/loved one has shared with you?

_____

_____

_____

_____

_____

_____

_____

_____

_____

_____

_____

_____

February 30

What changes would you like to make about what you are experiencing now?

_____

_____

_____

_____

_____

_____

_____

_____

_____

_____

_____

_____

March 9

Does your friend/loved one know how much you love him/her?

_____

_____

_____

_____

_____

_____

_____

_____

_____

_____

_____

_____

March 2

How important is being generous to others to you?

_____

_____

_____

_____

_____

_____

_____

_____

_____

_____

_____

_____

_____

March 3

Could you be more disciplined in managing your important responsibilities?

_____

_____

_____

_____

_____

_____

_____

_____

_____

_____

_____

March 4

What activities do you enjoy when you have free time?

_____

_____

_____

_____

_____

_____

_____

_____

_____

_____

_____

_____

_____

March 5

What was amazing about today?

_____

_____

_____

_____

_____

_____

_____

_____

_____

_____

_____

_____

_____

_____

March 6

Is your self-talk positive or negative?

_____
_____
_____
_____
_____
_____
_____
_____
_____
_____
_____
_____
_____
_____

March 7

How well do you communicate your ideas to others?

_____

_____

_____

_____

_____

_____

_____

_____

_____

_____

_____

_____

_____

March 8

Name five things you have achieved.

_____

_____

_____

_____

_____

_____

_____

_____

_____

_____

_____

_____

_____

_____

March 9

What would you like to improve about your home and why?

_____

_____

_____

_____

_____

_____

_____

_____

_____

_____

_____

_____

_____

March 10

What are you grateful for today?

_____

_____

_____

_____

_____

_____

_____

_____

_____

_____

_____

_____

_____

_____

March 11

Who is someone that has been gruel to you in your life? Have you forgiven him/her?

_____

_____

_____

_____

_____

_____

_____

_____

_____

_____

_____

_____

_____

March 12

What is some of the best advice your friend/loved one ever gave you?

_____

_____

_____

_____

_____

_____

_____

_____

_____

_____

_____

_____

_____

March 13

What would you like to re-experience again because you didn't appreciate it enough the first time?

_____

_____

_____

_____

_____

_____

_____

_____

_____

_____

_____

_____

March 14

What is a great mistake you have made and why?

_____

_____

_____

_____

_____

_____

_____

_____

_____

_____

_____

_____

_____

_____

March 15

Are you a people pleaser?

_____
_____
_____
_____
_____
_____
_____
_____
_____
_____
_____
_____
_____
_____

March 16

Do you wear perfume or cologne?

_____
_____
_____
_____
_____
_____
_____
_____
_____
_____
_____
_____
_____
_____

March 17

Why didn't you spend more time with...?

_____
_____
_____
_____
_____
_____
_____
_____
_____
_____
_____
_____
_____
_____

March 18

Think about compliments people have given you. What was your favorite one and why?

_____

_____

_____

_____

_____

_____

_____

_____

_____

_____

_____

_____

March 19

How do you feel about regrets? What type of regret will you try to avoid?

_____

_____

_____

_____

_____

_____

_____

_____

_____

_____

_____

_____

March 20

Do you have control issues?

_____
_____
_____
_____
_____
_____
_____
_____
_____
_____
_____
_____
_____
_____

March 29

What made today special?

_____

_____

_____

_____

_____

_____

_____

_____

_____

_____

_____

_____

_____

_____

_____

March 22

Is there anyone who might rightfully or wrongfully perceive me now to be meddling in their affairs?

_____

_____

_____

_____

_____

_____

_____

_____

_____

_____

_____

_____

March 23

Do you get in your own way?

_____

_____

_____

_____

_____

_____

_____

_____

_____

_____

_____

_____

_____

March 24

What do you consider a luxury?

_____

_____

_____

_____

_____

_____

_____

_____

_____

_____

_____

_____

_____

March 25

When was your last doctor's appointment?

_____

_____

_____

_____

_____

_____

_____

_____

_____

_____

_____

_____

_____

_____

March 26

Name three times in the past where you overcame an obstacle or in which you achieved success.

_____

_____

_____

_____

_____

_____

_____

_____

_____

_____

_____

_____

March 27

Have you been responsible for protecting your friend/loved one right now from potentially difficult people or situations? How?

_____
_____
_____
_____
_____
_____
_____
_____
_____
_____
_____
_____
_____

March 28

Suppose that someone you know came bursting through the door right now, out of breath, and he/she said they know your secret. Who is that person and what would they say?

_____

_____

_____

_____

_____

_____

_____

_____

_____

_____

_____

_____

_____

March 29

Have you ever been called difficult? By whom? Why?

_____
_____
_____
_____
_____
_____
_____
_____
_____
_____
_____
_____
_____
_____

March 30

Are you suffering grief that others can't understand and feel as though you must put on a brave face?

_____

_____

_____

_____

_____

_____

_____

_____

_____

_____

_____

_____

_____

March 31

What is one thing you could stop doing, or start doing, or do differently, starting today that would most improve the quality your life?

_____

_____

_____

_____

_____

_____

_____

_____

_____

_____

_____

_____

April 9

Is your work environment positive and supportive?

_____
_____
_____
_____
_____
_____
_____
_____
_____
_____
_____
_____
_____

April 2

How would you respond to a client who used rude or derogatory language toward you?

_____

_____

_____

_____

_____

_____

_____

_____

_____

_____

_____

_____

April 3

How important is prioritizing your responsibilities?

_____

_____

_____

_____

_____

_____

_____

_____

_____

_____

_____

_____

_____

_____

April 4

How emotionally healthy and strong do you currently feel?

_____

_____

_____

_____

_____

_____

_____

_____

_____

_____

_____

_____

_____

_____

April 5

What are your weaknesses?

_____

_____

_____

_____

_____

_____

_____

_____

_____

_____

_____

_____

_____

_____

April 6

When are you most productive in your day?

_____

_____

_____

_____

_____

_____

_____

_____

_____

_____

_____

_____

_____

April 7

If a client of yours refused to [take a shower, eat their meal, go to the bathroom, etc.], how would you deal with the situation?

_____

_____

_____

_____

_____

_____

_____

_____

_____

_____

_____

_____

April 8

Are you open to change?

_____

_____

_____

_____

_____

_____

_____

_____

_____

_____

_____

_____

_____

_____

April 9

What types of rewards best motivate you?

_____

_____

_____

_____

_____

_____

_____

_____

_____

_____

_____

_____

_____

_____

April 10

Do you follow your gut or intuition?

_____
_____
_____
_____
_____
_____
_____
_____
_____
_____
_____
_____
_____
_____
_____

April 11

What are the triggers that provoke you to do things you regret?

_____

_____

_____

_____

_____

_____

_____

_____

_____

_____

_____

_____

April 12

Do you need to socialize more or have more time alone?

_____
_____
_____
_____
_____
_____
_____
_____
_____
_____
_____
_____
_____
_____

April 13

What's the last thing you changed your mind about?

_____

_____

_____

_____

_____

_____

_____

_____

_____

_____

_____

_____

_____

April 14

What's on your mind right now?

_____

_____

_____

_____

_____

_____

_____

_____

_____

_____

_____

_____

_____

_____

_____

April 15

What's the best advice you've ever received?

_____

_____

_____

_____

_____

_____

_____

_____

_____

_____

_____

_____

_____

_____

April 16

What areas of your life are working well for you?

_____

_____

_____

_____

_____

_____

_____

_____

_____

_____

_____

_____

_____

_____

April 17

As a caregiver, how do you handle and monitor traffic to ensure that people don't over stay their welcome?

_____

_____

_____

_____

_____

_____

_____

_____

_____

_____

_____

_____

April 18

What skills or talents do you have that make you a better caregiver?

_____

_____

_____

_____

_____

_____

_____

_____

_____

_____

_____

_____

April 19

Consider a previous or current job- what specific activities have you done that you enjoy and find engaging?

_____
_____
_____
_____
_____
_____
_____
_____
_____
_____
_____
_____

April 20

How do you truly feel about the diagnosis of your friend/loved one?

_____

_____

_____

_____

_____

_____

_____

_____

_____

_____

_____

_____

April 29

Is the diagnosis clear to your friend or loved one?

_____

_____

_____

_____

_____

_____

_____

_____

_____

_____

_____

_____

_____

April 22

Are you able to understand and accept the diagnosis?

_____

_____

_____

_____

_____

_____

_____

_____

_____

_____

_____

_____

_____

_____

April 23

Do you ever feel "worn out"?

_____
_____
_____
_____
_____
_____
_____
_____
_____
_____
_____
_____
_____
_____

April 24

What's your favorite go-to recipe for a quick and satisfying meal?

_____

_____

_____

_____

_____

_____

_____

_____

_____

_____

_____

_____

_____

April 25

In what skills area do you feel most qualified to be a caregiver and in what area of skill do you feel the least qualified to be a caregiver?

_____

_____

_____

_____

_____

_____

_____

_____

_____

_____

_____

_____

April 26

Are there ways in which you tend not to want to be honest, either in your words or in your actions?

_____

_____

_____

_____

_____

_____

_____

_____

_____

_____

_____

April 27

What are your favorite card and board games to play?

_____

_____

_____

_____

_____

_____

_____

_____

_____

_____

_____

_____

_____

April 28

During an average week, how much of your time is spent doing things you dislike or that you feel waste your time?

_____

_____

_____

_____

_____

_____

_____

_____

_____

_____

_____

_____

_____

April 29

Do you have any guilty pleasures that may have a potential of becoming toxic or addictive?

_____

_____

_____

_____

_____

_____

_____

_____

_____

_____

_____

_____

_____

April 30

If you have any questions about the care of your friend/loved one, who might help you?

_____

_____

_____

_____

_____

_____

_____

_____

_____

_____

_____

_____

May 1

How do you spend your weekends?

_____

_____

_____

_____

_____

_____

_____

_____

_____

_____

_____

_____

_____

_____

May 2

Is there anything that you must protect your friend/loved one from?

_____

_____

_____

_____

_____

_____

_____

_____

_____

_____

_____

_____

May 3

How satisfied are you with your current home environment?

_____

_____

_____

_____

_____

_____

_____

_____

_____

_____

_____

_____

_____

_____

May 4

Are you confident and secure in who you are as a caregiver?

_____
_____
_____
_____
_____
_____
_____
_____
_____
_____
_____
_____
_____
_____

May 5

Have you talked about death with your friend or loved one?

_____
_____
_____
_____
_____
_____
_____
_____
_____
_____
_____
_____
_____
_____

May 6

Are you a good listener?

_____

_____

_____

_____

_____

_____

_____

_____

_____

_____

_____

_____

_____

May 7

Do you ever feel selfish? Is it really justified?

_____
_____
_____
_____
_____
_____
_____
_____
_____
_____
_____
_____

May 8

What do you want to accomplish today?

_____

_____

_____

_____

_____

_____

_____

_____

_____

_____

_____

_____

_____

_____

May 9

Are you the only caregiver or main caregiver for your friend/loved one?

_____

_____

_____

_____

_____

_____

_____

_____

_____

_____

_____

_____

May 10

Is there anything that you are pretending to know?

_____

_____

_____

_____

_____

_____

_____

_____

_____

_____

_____

_____

May 11

If you have help caring for your loved one, does s/he have the names, addresses and emergency phone numbers of the other caregivers (i.e., family, friends, neighbors, home care services, etc.)?

_____

_____

_____

_____

_____

_____

_____

_____

_____

_____

_____

_____

_____

May 12

Do you ever feel like you can't leave your friend/loved one alone?

_____

_____

_____

_____

_____

_____

_____

_____

_____

_____

_____

May 13

Have you ever lost sleep due to your caregiver role?

_____
_____
_____
_____
_____
_____
_____
_____
_____
_____
_____
_____
_____
_____

May 14

Do you have a lot of personal photos of your friend/loved one?

_____

_____

_____

_____

_____

_____

_____

_____

_____

_____

_____

_____

May 15

Do you need an alarm clock to wake up in the morning?

_____

_____

_____

_____

_____

_____

_____

_____

_____

_____

_____

_____

May 16

Have you engaged in activities like drugs, alcohol, over or under-eating, or other disruptive behaviors to avoid feeling tired, stressed or anxious?

_____

_____

_____

_____

_____

_____

_____

_____

_____

_____

_____

_____

_____

May 17

Have you ever thought your friend/loved one's living situation to be inconvenient or a barrier to good care?

_____

_____

_____

_____

_____

_____

_____

_____

_____

_____

_____

_____

May 18

How many hours per week do you spend checking email?
Watching TV? Surfing the Net? Social Media?

_____

_____

_____

_____

_____

_____

_____

_____

_____

_____

_____

_____

May 19

Have you ever felt that your friend/loved one asks for more help than they need?

_____

_____

_____

_____

_____

_____

_____

_____

_____

_____

_____

May 20

What is the last book you've read?

_____

_____

_____

_____

_____

_____

_____

_____

_____

_____

_____

_____

_____

May 21

Do you feel stressed between taking care of your
friend/loved one and trying to meet the responsibilities of
your family?

_____

_____

_____

_____

_____

_____

_____

_____

_____

_____

_____

_____

_____

May 22

Have you ever felt embarrassed by your friend/loved one's behavior?

_____

_____

_____

_____

_____

_____

_____

_____

_____

_____

_____

_____

May 23

Do you have a meditation practice?

_____
_____
_____
_____
_____
_____
_____
_____
_____
_____
_____
_____
_____
_____

May 24

Do you ever feel angry around your friend/loved one?

_____
_____
_____
_____
_____
_____
_____
_____
_____
_____
_____
_____
_____

May 25

Do you feel that your friend/loved one affects your relationships with other family members or friends in a negative way?

_____

_____

_____

_____

_____

_____

_____

_____

_____

_____

_____

May 26

How do you handle stress?

_____

_____

_____

_____

_____

_____

_____

_____

_____

_____

_____

_____

_____

_____

May 27

Are you afraid of what the future holds for your friend/ loved one?

_____

_____

_____

_____

_____

_____

_____

_____

_____

_____

_____

_____

May 28

Do you feel your friend/ loved one is dependent on you?

_____

_____

_____

_____

_____

_____

_____

_____

_____

_____

_____

_____

_____

_____

May 29

What was the last compliment someone gave you? What was the last compliment you gave someone else?

_____

_____

_____

_____

_____

_____

_____

_____

_____

_____

_____

_____

_____

May 30

Do you feel your health has suffered because of your involvement with your friend/loved one?

_____

_____

_____

_____

_____

_____

_____

_____

_____

_____

_____

_____

May 31

Do you feel that you don't have as much privacy as you would like because of your friend/loved one's situation?

_____

_____

_____

_____

_____

_____

_____

_____

_____

_____

_____

_____

June 9

Do you feel that your social life has suffered because you are caring for your friend/loved one?

_____
_____
_____
_____
_____
_____
_____
_____
_____
_____
_____
_____

June 2

How willing are you to step out of your comfort zone?

_____
_____
_____
_____
_____
_____
_____
_____
_____
_____
_____
_____
_____

June 3

Do you feel uncomfortable about having friends to your home because of your friend/loved one?

_____

_____

_____

_____

_____

_____

_____

_____

_____

_____

_____

_____

_____

_____

June 4

How fulfilled are you with the way in which you're currently living your life?

_____

_____

_____

_____

_____

_____

_____

_____

_____

_____

_____

_____

_____

June 5

Do you feel that your friend/loved one seems to expect you to take care of them as if you were the only one they could depend on?

_____

_____

_____

_____

_____

_____

_____

_____

_____

_____

_____

_____

June 6

How do you feel around negative people?

_____

_____

_____

_____

_____

_____

_____

_____

_____

_____

_____

_____

_____

June 7

Do you talk to yourself?

_____
_____
_____
_____
_____
_____
_____
_____
_____
_____
_____
_____
_____
_____
_____

June 8

Are you kind to yourself?

_____

_____

_____

_____

_____

_____

_____

_____

_____

_____

_____

_____

_____

_____

June 9

Under what circumstances do you ever find yourself angry?

_____

_____

_____

_____

_____

_____

_____

_____

_____

_____

_____

_____

_____

June 10

Do you feel that you do not have enough money to take care of your friend/loved one in addition to your other expenses?

_____

_____

_____

_____

_____

_____

_____

_____

_____

_____

_____

_____

June 11

Do you have a secret?

_____
_____
_____
_____
_____
_____
_____
_____
_____
_____
_____
_____
_____

June 12

Do you feel you have lost control of your life since your friend/relative became ill?

_____

_____

_____

_____

_____

_____

_____

_____

_____

_____

_____

_____

June 13

Is there something you wish you had said to someone but didn't get the chance?

_____
_____
_____
_____
_____
_____
_____
_____
_____
_____
_____
_____

June 14

Do you ever wish you could leave the care of your loved one to someone else?

_____
_____
_____
_____
_____
_____
_____
_____
_____
_____
_____
_____
_____

June 15

Do you feel uncertain about what to do about your loved one?

_____

_____

_____

_____

_____

_____

_____

_____

_____

_____

_____

_____

_____

June 16

Do you ever feel you should be doing more for your loved one?

_____
_____
_____
_____
_____
_____
_____
_____
_____
_____
_____
_____
_____

June 17

Do you feel that you could do a better job of caring for your loved one?

_____

_____

_____

_____

_____

_____

_____

_____

_____

_____

_____

June 18

Overall, how burdened do you feel in caring for your friend/loved one?

_____
_____
_____
_____
_____
_____
_____
_____
_____
_____
_____
_____

June 19

Do you ever have trouble keeping your mind on what you are doing?

_____
_____
_____
_____
_____
_____
_____
_____
_____
_____
_____
_____
_____

June 20

Do you have any difficulty making decisions?

_____

_____

_____

_____

_____

_____

_____

_____

_____

_____

_____

_____

_____

_____

June 21

Have you ever had a crying spell?

_____

_____

_____

_____

_____

_____

_____

_____

_____

_____

_____

_____

June 22

Do you exercise on a regular basis?

_____
_____
_____
_____
_____
_____
_____
_____
_____
_____
_____
_____
_____

June 23

Do you make and keep preventive and necessary medical and dental appointments for yourself?

_____

_____

_____

_____

_____

_____

_____

_____

_____

_____

_____

_____

_____

June 24

Do you have at least one person in whom you can confide (tell your problems, discuss your successes)?

_____

_____

_____

_____

_____

_____

_____

_____

_____

_____

_____

_____

_____

June 25

Do you take time to do things that are important to you (e.g., church, garden, read, spend time alone)?

_____

_____

_____

_____

_____

_____

_____

_____

_____

_____

_____

_____

_____

June 26

Have you ever felt resentful?

_____

_____

_____

_____

_____

_____

_____

_____

_____

_____

_____

_____

_____

_____

June 27

On a scale of one to ten, how healthy are you?

_____

_____

_____

_____

_____

_____

_____

_____

_____

_____

_____

_____

_____

_____

_____

June 28

Have you ever felt drained or helpless?

_____

_____

_____

_____

_____

_____

_____

_____

_____

_____

_____

_____

_____

June 29

Have you ever been upset that your friend/ relative has changed so much from his/her former self?

_____

_____

_____

_____

_____

_____

_____

_____

_____

_____

_____

_____

June 30

How long have you been a caregiver of your friend/loved one?

_____

_____

_____

_____

_____

_____

_____

_____

_____

_____

_____

July 9

Does your friend/relative need help with activities of daily living?

_____

_____

_____

_____

_____

_____

_____

_____

_____

_____

_____

_____

July 2

How much do you worry about your current financial situation?

_____

_____

_____

_____

_____

_____

_____

_____

_____

_____

_____

_____

July 3

Would your home life be easier if you had a better system in place for managing your routine responsibilities? How?

_____

_____

_____

_____

_____

_____

_____

_____

_____

_____

_____

_____

_____

_____

July 4

How spiritually healthy do you currently feel?

_____

_____

_____

_____

_____

_____

_____

_____

_____

_____

_____

_____

_____

_____

_____

July 5

Does your friend/loved one need specialized care (physical therapy, wound care)?

_____

_____

_____

_____

_____

_____

_____

_____

_____

_____

_____

_____

July 6

What motivates you?

_____
_____
_____
_____
_____
_____
_____
_____
_____
_____
_____
_____
_____
_____

July 7

What's your preferred style of communication: verbal or nonverbal?

_____

_____

_____

_____

_____

_____

_____

_____

_____

_____

_____

_____

July 8

Do you reward yourself when you accomplish tasks?

_____

_____

_____

_____

_____

_____

_____

_____

_____

_____

_____

_____

_____

July 9

Are you also providing care to other individuals?

_____

_____

_____

_____

_____

_____

_____

_____

_____

_____

_____

_____

_____

July 10

What's your favorite question to ask people?

_____

_____

_____

_____

_____

_____

_____

_____

_____

_____

_____

_____

_____

July 11

Is there anyone else you can call on in an emergency to fill in for you as caregiver?

_____

_____

_____

_____

_____

_____

_____

_____

_____

_____

_____

July 12

Do you feel obligated to be your friend/relative's caregiver?

_____

_____

_____

_____

_____

_____

_____

_____

_____

_____

_____

_____

_____

July 13

What choice are you thankful that you did not make?

_____

_____

_____

_____

_____

_____

_____

_____

_____

_____

_____

_____

_____

July 14

Have you begun to think about how you plan to provide care for the individual in the long-term future?

_____

_____

_____

_____

_____

_____

_____

_____

_____

_____

_____

_____

July 15

What is a problem you solved today?

_____

_____

_____

_____

_____

_____

_____

_____

_____

_____

_____

_____

_____

July 16

In the event you pass away or are unable to provide care for other reasons, have you begun to think about who else could or will provide care in the future?

_____

_____

_____

_____

_____

_____

_____

_____

_____

_____

_____

_____

_____

July 17

Have you begun to think about what other supports will be needed to provide care in the future? This could include the option for a residential placement (from a group home to independent living, bringing additional supports in to your home, etc.).

_____

_____

_____

_____

_____

_____

_____

_____

_____

_____

July 18

How would you describe your social support system?

_____
_____
_____
_____
_____
_____
_____
_____
_____
_____
_____
_____
_____
_____

July 19

What is the most stressful aspect of caregiving for you?

_____
_____
_____
_____
_____
_____
_____
_____
_____
_____
_____
_____
_____
_____

July 20

What is working well in your caregiving situation?

_____

_____

_____

_____

_____

_____

_____

_____

_____

_____

_____

_____

_____

_____

July 21

What is one important lesson you have learned and can recommend to other caregivers?

_____

_____

_____

_____

_____

_____

_____

_____

_____

_____

_____

_____

_____

July 22

When's the last time you had a belly laugh?

_____
_____
_____
_____
_____
_____
_____
_____
_____
_____
_____
_____
_____

July 23

Have you used community resources to help in the care of your friend/loved one?

_____

_____

_____

_____

_____

_____

_____

_____

_____

_____

_____

_____

July 24

Do you have a favorite quote?

_____
_____
_____
_____
_____
_____
_____
_____
_____
_____
_____
_____
_____
_____

July 25

How's the emotional health of your friend/ loved one?

_____
_____
_____
_____
_____
_____
_____
_____
_____
_____
_____
_____
_____

July 26

What do you consider to be your biggest achievement?

_____
_____
_____
_____
_____
_____
_____
_____
_____
_____
_____
_____
_____

Jul 27

Do you wear a watch?

_____
_____
_____
_____
_____
_____
_____
_____
_____
_____
_____
_____
_____
_____
_____

July 28

Do you participate in a caregiver support group?

_____

_____

_____

_____

_____

_____

_____

_____

_____

_____

_____

_____

_____

_____

July 29

How are other family members involved in caregiving of your friend/ relative?

_____

_____

_____

_____

_____

_____

_____

_____

_____

_____

_____

_____

July 30

How has your relationship with the care receiver changed?

_____
_____
_____
_____
_____
_____
_____
_____
_____
_____
_____
_____
_____
_____

July 31

What is the most difficult aspect of caregiving for you?

_____

_____

_____

_____

_____

_____

_____

_____

_____

_____

_____

_____

_____

_____

August 9

Do you have a healthy and rewarding work/life balance?

_____
_____
_____
_____
_____
_____
_____
_____
_____
_____
_____
_____

August 2

How important is establishing personal and professional boundaries to you?

_____

_____

_____

_____

_____

_____

_____

_____

_____

_____

_____

_____

_____

_____

August 3

How much do you worry about your routine responsibilities?

_____

_____

_____

_____

_____

_____

_____

_____

_____

_____

_____

_____

_____

_____

August 4

What is working well in your caregiving situation?

_____

_____

_____

_____

_____

_____

_____

_____

_____

_____

_____

_____

August 5

What are the current community resources that you use?

_____
_____
_____
_____
_____
_____
_____
_____
_____
_____
_____
_____
_____
_____
_____

August 6

What keeps you going?

_____

_____

_____

_____

_____

_____

_____

_____

_____

_____

_____

_____

_____

_____

August 7

Are you a good listener?

_____
_____
_____
_____
_____
_____
_____
_____
_____
_____
_____
_____
_____
_____

August 8

What is your normal work week?

_____

_____

_____

_____

_____

_____

_____

_____

_____

_____

_____

_____

_____

_____

_____

August 9

What is the care receiver's current health status, illnesses, and disabilities?

_____

_____

_____

_____

_____

_____

_____

_____

_____

_____

_____

_____

_____

_____

August 10

Who has been your closest friend?

_____
_____
_____
_____
_____
_____
_____
_____
_____
_____
_____
_____
_____
_____

August 11

What health issues cause you the greatest concern for your friend/relative and why?

_____

_____

_____

_____

_____

_____

_____

_____

_____

_____

_____

_____

_____

August 12

How would you describe your faith?

_____
_____
_____
_____
_____
_____
_____
_____
_____
_____
_____
_____
_____
_____
_____

August 13

What do you know about your friend/relative's disease/situation and how it affects the body?

_____

_____

_____

_____

_____

_____

_____

_____

_____

_____

_____

_____

August 14

What bothered you today?

_____

_____

_____

_____

_____

_____

_____

_____

_____

_____

_____

_____

_____

_____

August 15

Do you need to seek more outside help with personal or professional care needs?

_____

_____

_____

_____

_____

_____

_____

_____

_____

_____

_____

_____

_____

August 16

How ambitious do you feel today?

_____
_____
_____
_____
_____
_____
_____
_____
_____
_____
_____
_____
_____

August 17

What details from today would you like to remember?

_____

_____

_____

_____

_____

_____

_____

_____

_____

_____

_____

_____

_____

_____

August 18

When's the last time you had a good cry?

_____

_____

_____

_____

_____

_____

_____

_____

_____

_____

_____

_____

_____

_____

_____

August 19

Share a fond memory of you and your friend/relative before the illness/situation.

_____
_____
_____
_____
_____
_____
_____
_____
_____
_____
_____
_____

August 20

On a scale of one to ten, how spontaneous were you today?

_____

_____

_____

_____

_____

_____

_____

_____

_____

_____

_____

_____

_____

_____

August 29

How do you relate to your friend/loved one now and how do you show your compassion support?

_____

_____

_____

_____

_____

_____

_____

_____

_____

_____

_____

_____

_____

August 22

Does your friend/loved one ever leave the home (i.e., to visit a senior center, for social reasons, to attend church, etc.)? If so, when?

_____

_____

_____

_____

_____

_____

_____

_____

_____

_____

_____

_____

August 23

Are you quiet or talkative?

_____
_____
_____
_____
_____
_____
_____
_____
_____
_____
_____
_____

August 24

What are your expectations for vacation time, and are you willing to help find coverage for the days that you need to take off?

_____

_____

_____

_____

_____

_____

_____

_____

_____

_____

_____

_____

August 25

What plan can you make to spruce up your friend/loved one's room to make it feel more joyful?

_____

_____

_____

_____

_____

_____

_____

_____

_____

_____

_____

_____

_____

August 26

Who is the last person you talked with on your cell phone?

_____

_____

_____

_____

_____

_____

_____

_____

_____

_____

_____

_____

_____

_____

August 27

Have you ever cared for someone with [conditions relatable to your loved one's care: memory problems, elderly, wheelchair bound, etc.] before?

_____

_____

_____

_____

_____

_____

_____

_____

_____

_____

_____

_____

_____

August 28

What's something interesting about you that most people may not know?

_____

_____

_____

_____

_____

_____

_____

_____

_____

_____

_____

_____

August 29

What's been one of your biggest challenges?

_____

_____

_____

_____

_____

_____

_____

_____

_____

_____

_____

_____

_____

August 30

Do you have any CPR or first-aid training?

_____

_____

_____

_____

_____

_____

_____

_____

_____

_____

_____

_____

_____

August 31

What's a life lesson that's benefitted you?

_____

_____

_____

_____

_____

_____

_____

_____

_____

_____

_____

_____

_____

September 9

How would you respond to care refusal?

_____
_____
_____
_____
_____
_____
_____
_____
_____
_____
_____
_____
_____

September 2

Do you keep daily records, and how do you keep others in the family informed?

_____

_____

_____

_____

_____

_____

_____

_____

_____

_____

_____

_____

_____

September 3

What kind of hobbies or interests do you have?

_____
_____
_____
_____
_____
_____
_____
_____
_____
_____
_____
_____

September 4

How consistent are you at managing your emotions?

_____
_____
_____
_____
_____
_____
_____
_____
_____
_____
_____
_____
_____

September 5

What are you denying about yourself or your life?

_____
_____
_____
_____
_____
_____
_____
_____
_____
_____
_____
_____
_____

September 6

Do you find yourself worrying when your mind is idle?

_____
_____
_____
_____
_____
_____
_____
_____
_____
_____
_____
_____
_____

September 7

What kind of hobbies or interests do you have?

_____

_____

_____

_____

_____

_____

_____

_____

_____

_____

_____

_____

_____

September 8

What physical and emotional changes have you observed in your friend/loved one?

_____

_____

_____

_____

_____

_____

_____

_____

_____

_____

_____

_____

September 9

What did you do or needs to be done to make the care receiver's space safer?

_____

_____

_____

_____

_____

_____

_____

_____

_____

_____

_____

_____

September 10

What gives you peace of mind?

_____

_____

_____

_____

_____

_____

_____

_____

_____

_____

_____

_____

_____

_____

September 11

Do you have caregiving experience with geriatric patients?

_____

_____

_____

_____

_____

_____

_____

_____

_____

_____

_____

_____

September 12

Do you believe that caregivers need medical training?

_____
_____
_____
_____
_____
_____
_____
_____
_____
_____
_____
_____
_____

September 13

Describe a cherished memory.

_____

_____

_____

_____

_____

_____

_____

_____

_____

_____

_____

_____

_____

_____

September 14

How are you handling medical emergencies?

_____

_____

_____

_____

_____

_____

_____

_____

_____

_____

_____

_____

_____

September 15

How could today have been better?

_____

_____

_____

_____

_____

_____

_____

_____

_____

_____

_____

_____

_____

September 16

What aspect of caregiving can get you down or discourage you?

_____

_____

_____

_____

_____

_____

_____

_____

_____

_____

_____

_____

September 17

What is a particular experience where you felt like you made a difference in the life of your friend/loved one?

_____

_____

_____

_____

_____

_____

_____

_____

_____

_____

_____

_____

September 18

What's on your to-do list?

_____

_____

_____

_____

_____

_____

_____

_____

_____

_____

_____

_____

_____

September 19

How do you practice self-care?

_____

_____

_____

_____

_____

_____

_____

_____

_____

_____

_____

_____

September 20

How do you handle the pressure of being your friend/loved one's caregiver?

_____

_____

_____

_____

_____

_____

_____

_____

_____

_____

_____

_____

_____

September 29

What do you try to avoid?

_____

_____

_____

_____

_____

_____

_____

_____

_____

_____

_____

_____

_____

_____

September 22

What do you love about your life?

_____

_____

_____

_____

_____

_____

_____

_____

_____

_____

_____

_____

_____

September 23

What did you get done today?

_____

_____

_____

_____

_____

_____

_____

_____

_____

_____

_____

_____

September 24

How do you handle people that are angry, annoyed, or afraid?

_____

_____

_____

_____

_____

_____

_____

_____

_____

_____

_____

_____

September 25

What's a new habit you want to adopt?

_____

_____

_____

_____

_____

_____

_____

_____

_____

_____

_____

_____

_____

_____

September 26

Do you have a gratitude practice?

_____
_____
_____
_____
_____
_____
_____
_____
_____
_____
_____
_____
_____
_____

September 27

What's unique about you?

_____

_____

_____

_____

_____

_____

_____

_____

_____

_____

_____

_____

_____

_____

September 28

List three things that made you smile today.

_____

_____

_____

_____

_____

_____

_____

_____

_____

_____

_____

_____

_____

September 29

What's an area of your life that you would like to improve?

_____
_____
_____
_____
_____
_____
_____
_____
_____
_____
_____
_____

September 30

What is one positive change you have already made this year?

_____

_____

_____

_____

_____

_____

_____

_____

_____

_____

_____

_____

October 9

What is one adjustment you would like to make to your morning routine?

_____

_____

_____

_____

_____

_____

_____

_____

_____

_____

_____

_____

October 2

How happy are you with your current physical fitness levels?

_____
_____
_____
_____
_____
_____
_____
_____
_____
_____
_____
_____
_____

October 3

What is one problem you had today, and what was your solution to this problem?
Was it the best way you could have handled it?

_____

_____

_____

_____

_____

_____

_____

_____

_____

_____

_____

_____

_____

October 4

What are the main challenges (or difficulties) that you're currently facing in life?

_____

_____

_____

_____

_____

_____

_____

_____

_____

_____

_____

_____

_____

October 5

List five good things about today.

_____
_____
_____
_____
_____
_____
_____
_____
_____
_____
_____
_____

October 6

What is it to be passionate? What are you passionate about?

_____
_____
_____
_____
_____
_____
_____
_____
_____
_____
_____
_____
_____
_____

October 7

Are you always honest with yourself?

_____
_____
_____
_____
_____
_____
_____
_____
_____
_____
_____
_____
_____
_____
_____

October 8

How well do you focus on tasks?

_____

_____

_____

_____

_____

_____

_____

_____

_____

_____

_____

_____

_____

_____

October 9

Did you allow yourself time to relax today?

_____
_____
_____
_____
_____
_____
_____
_____
_____
_____
_____
_____
_____

October 10

What are your favorite memories of your friend/relative?

_____
_____
_____
_____
_____
_____
_____
_____
_____
_____
_____
_____
_____

October 11

What's something that is important for you to remember when you are faced with a difficult situation?

_____

_____

_____

_____

_____

_____

_____

_____

_____

_____

_____

October 12

Describe a magical experience.

_____
_____
_____
_____
_____
_____
_____
_____
_____
_____
_____
_____
_____
_____
_____

October 13

What are you most proud of?

_____

_____

_____

_____

_____

_____

_____

_____

_____

_____

_____

_____

_____

October 14

Today, my victories included:

_____

_____

_____

_____

_____

_____

_____

_____

_____

_____

_____

_____

_____

_____

_____

October 15

How did you spend your day?

_____

_____

_____

_____

_____

_____

_____

_____

_____

_____

_____

_____

_____

October 16

If you could have a superpower just for today, what would it be?

_____

_____

_____

_____

_____

_____

_____

_____

_____

_____

_____

_____

October 17

What's your favorite thing to do on a rainy day?

_____

_____

_____

_____

_____

_____

_____

_____

_____

_____

_____

_____

_____

October 18

What are you grateful for today?

_____
_____
_____
_____
_____
_____
_____
_____
_____
_____
_____
_____
_____
_____

October 19

Even when I'm overwhelmed, stressed or upset, I can't help but smile or laugh when I see _____ because...

_____

_____

_____

_____

_____

_____

_____

_____

_____

_____

_____

_____

October 20

What is a decision you made today?

_____

_____

_____

_____

_____

_____

_____

_____

_____

_____

_____

_____

_____

October 29

What is the source of your current stress?

_____

_____

_____

_____

_____

_____

_____

_____

_____

_____

_____

_____

_____

October 22

What is the most important thing you should accomplish in the next 24 hours?

_____

_____

_____

_____

_____

_____

_____

_____

_____

_____

_____

_____

October 23

When's the last time you took a nap?

_____

_____

_____

_____

_____

_____

_____

_____

_____

_____

_____

_____

_____

October 24

What new activity have you tried?

_____
_____
_____
_____
_____
_____
_____
_____
_____
_____
_____
_____

October 25

How do you want to be remembered?

_____
_____
_____
_____
_____
_____
_____
_____
_____
_____
_____
_____
_____
_____

October 26

If you could change one thing about today, what would it be?

_____

_____

_____

_____

_____

_____

_____

_____

_____

_____

_____

_____

_____

October 27

How many steps do you average per day?

_____

_____

_____

_____

_____

_____

_____

_____

_____

_____

_____

_____

October 28

What question(s) do you hate to answer?

_____

_____

_____

_____

_____

_____

_____

_____

_____

_____

_____

_____

_____

_____

October 29

What did you have difficulty coping with today?

_____

_____

_____

_____

_____

_____

_____

_____

_____

_____

_____

_____

_____

_____

October 30

In three words, describe your day. Why these words?

_____
_____
_____
_____
_____
_____
_____
_____
_____
_____
_____
_____
_____

October 31

Is there anything you need to accept or make peace with?

_____
_____
_____
_____
_____
_____
_____
_____
_____
_____
_____
_____
_____
_____

November 9

What self-care did you practice for yourself today?

_____

_____

_____

_____

_____

_____

_____

_____

_____

_____

_____

_____

_____

November 2

How content are you with the amount of free time you have?

_____

_____

_____

_____

_____

_____

_____

_____

_____

_____

_____

_____

_____

_____

November 3

How do you regularly make a positive impact in the lives of other people?

_____

_____

_____

_____

_____

_____

_____

_____

_____

_____

_____

November 4

What is working really well in your life at this stage of your life?

_____

_____

_____

_____

_____

_____

_____

_____

_____

_____

_____

_____

November 5

What past hurts and sufferings do you need to let go?
Acknowledge what you have learned along the way.

_____

_____

_____

_____

_____

_____

_____

_____

_____

_____

_____

_____

November 6

What actions are you avoiding?

_____
_____
_____
_____
_____
_____
_____
_____
_____
_____
_____
_____
_____
_____

November 7

How do you let go of fear when you are in a challenging situation?

_____

_____

_____

_____

_____

_____

_____

_____

_____

_____

_____

_____

_____

_____

November 8

Do you have any unfinished tasks/projects?

_____

_____

_____

_____

_____

_____

_____

_____

_____

_____

_____

_____

_____

November 9

What's a lesson you learned this week?

_____
_____
_____
_____
_____
_____
_____
_____
_____
_____
_____
_____
_____
_____

November 10

What are five things that made you smile today?

_____
_____
_____
_____
_____
_____
_____
_____
_____
_____
_____
_____
_____

November 11

Do you need to make any adjustments to your evening routine?

_____

_____

_____

_____

_____

_____

_____

_____

_____

_____

_____

_____

November 12

Who is the wisest person you know?

_____
_____
_____
_____
_____
_____
_____
_____
_____
_____
_____
_____
_____
_____

November 13

Do you have any memorable stories about your family members?

_____

_____

_____

_____

_____

_____

_____

_____

_____

_____

_____

_____

_____

November 14

What did you learn today?

_____
_____
_____
_____
_____
_____
_____
_____
_____
_____
_____
_____
_____

November 15

What did you do for physical activity today?

_____

_____

_____

_____

_____

_____

_____

_____

_____

_____

_____

_____

_____

_____

November 16

How do you get out of a rut?

_____
_____
_____
_____
_____
_____
_____
_____
_____
_____
_____
_____
_____
_____

November 17

What kinds of activities and hobbies does your friend/loved one enjoy? What are his/her favorite shows, books, magazines, etc.?

_____

_____

_____

_____

_____

_____

_____

_____

_____

_____

_____

_____

_____

November 18

What is something you have that has improved the quality of your life?

_____

_____

_____

_____

_____

_____

_____

_____

_____

_____

_____

_____

_____

November 19

Does your loved one have special dietary needs that must be taken into consideration? If so, can s/he still go to the grocery store alone? Does s/he need assistance shopping for items to meet those dietary needs?

_____

_____

_____

_____

_____

_____

_____

_____

_____

_____

_____

_____

November 20

How do you show others that you appreciate them?

_____

_____

_____

_____

_____

_____

_____

_____

_____

_____

_____

_____

November 29

What's an unforgettable experience you've had?

_____

_____

_____

_____

_____

_____

_____

_____

_____

_____

_____

_____

_____

November 22

Are your loved one's living quarters secure? Does s/he have the ability to evade unwelcomed visitors (i.e., scammers, solicitors, etc.)?

_____

_____

_____

_____

_____

_____

_____

_____

_____

_____

_____

_____

November 23

How comfortable are you performing the necessary tasks to care for your loved one?

_____

_____

_____

_____

_____

_____

_____

_____

_____

_____

_____

November 24

How do you prioritize your time?

_____
_____
_____
_____
_____
_____
_____
_____
_____
_____
_____
_____
_____
_____

November 25

How would you work with your friend/relative who is non-verbal or unable to communicate?

_____

_____

_____

_____

_____

_____

_____

_____

_____

_____

_____

_____

November 26

What are you grateful for today?

_____

_____

_____

_____

_____

_____

_____

_____

_____

_____

_____

_____

_____

November 27

When is the last time you had an inspiring conversation?

_____

_____

_____

_____

_____

_____

_____

_____

_____

_____

_____

_____

_____

_____

November 28

How did you make a difference in your loved one's life today?

_____
_____
_____
_____
_____
_____
_____
_____
_____
_____
_____
_____
_____

November 29

What current event or issue do you feel very strongly about?

_____

_____

_____

_____

_____

_____

_____

_____

_____

_____

_____

_____

_____

_____

November 30

Write a positive affirmation for yourself.

_____

_____

_____

_____

_____

_____

_____

_____

_____

_____

_____

_____

December 9

Do you know the difference between feelings of

pity and feelings of compassion?

_____

_____

_____

_____

_____

_____

_____

_____

_____

_____

_____

_____

December 2

Looking back at your relationship with your relative, what are some of the ways in which you might still be harbouring feelings of resentment, abandonment, or fear of loss of control?

_____

_____

_____

_____

_____

_____

_____

_____

_____

_____

_____

_____

December 3

How important is leaving behind a meaningful legacy to you?

_____

_____

_____

_____

_____

_____

_____

_____

_____

_____

_____

_____

_____

_____

December 4

What would it take for your life to feel more effectively balanced?

_____

_____

_____

_____

_____

_____

_____

_____

_____

_____

_____

_____

December 5

What expectations do you have for yourself and your life?

_____

_____

_____

_____

_____

_____

_____

_____

_____

_____

_____

_____

December 6

What is your attention on today?

_____

_____

_____

_____

_____

_____

_____

_____

_____

_____

_____

_____

_____

December 7

Have you ever done something you were told you couldn't do?

_____

_____

_____

_____

_____

_____

_____

_____

_____

_____

_____

_____

_____

December 8

What are three words to describe your social life? Why?

_____

_____

_____

_____

_____

_____

_____

_____

_____

_____

_____

_____

_____

_____

December 9

What personal and professional goals do you want to set for the coming new year?

_____

_____

_____

_____

_____

_____

_____

_____

_____

_____

_____

_____

December 10

Did you ever have car trouble at a particularly inconvenient time?

_____

_____

_____

_____

_____

_____

_____

_____

_____

_____

_____

_____

December 11

What's a recurring dream you have?

_____
_____
_____
_____
_____
_____
_____
_____
_____
_____
_____
_____
_____

December 12

What is something that most people would be surprised to know about you?

_____

_____

_____

_____

_____

_____

_____

_____

_____

_____

_____

_____

_____

December 13

What is something unusual that you own?

_____
_____
_____
_____
_____
_____
_____
_____
_____
_____
_____
_____
_____

December 14

List three things you do regularly that are good for your
health. Write about how each one helps you.

_____

_____

_____

_____

_____

_____

_____

_____

_____

_____

_____

_____

_____

December 15

What types of rules about food did your family have when you were growing up? How did those rules affect you?

_____

_____

_____

_____

_____

_____

_____

_____

_____

_____

_____

_____

_____

_____

December 16

What health concerns do you think you may have when you
get older? How can you begin to address them now?

_____

_____

_____

_____

_____

_____

_____

_____

_____

_____

_____

_____

December 17

Do you know what screenings and appointments are recommended for someone your age?

_____

_____

_____

_____

_____

_____

_____

_____

_____

_____

_____

_____

December 18

Do you live a sedentary or active lifestyle? What could you do to be more active?

_____

_____

_____

_____

_____

_____

_____

_____

_____

_____

_____

_____

_____

_____

December 19

Do you have holiday traditions? Any favorites?

_____

_____

_____

_____

_____

_____

_____

_____

_____

_____

_____

_____

_____

_____

December 20

What do you like to do to improve your mood when you're having a bad day?

_____

_____

_____

_____

_____

_____

_____

_____

_____

_____

_____

_____

_____

December 29

What's on your wish list?

_____

_____

_____

_____

_____

_____

_____

_____

_____

_____

_____

_____

_____

_____

December 22

What things do you do that are good for your mental health?

_____

_____

_____

_____

_____

_____

_____

_____

_____

_____

_____

_____

_____

December 24

The things that help me the most right now are...

_____
_____
_____
_____
_____
_____
_____
_____
_____
_____
_____
_____
_____

December 25

What are you sentimental about?

_____
_____
_____
_____
_____
_____
_____
_____
_____
_____
_____
_____
_____
_____
_____

December 26

If you could choose any place or scenario (real or imaginary) to place yourself in right now for your comfort and relaxation, where would it be? Describe it in as much detail as possible.

_____

_____

_____

_____

_____

_____

_____

_____

_____

_____

_____

December 27

Write about all the places that you can currently feel tension in your body. Write about all the areas that feel relaxed.

_____

_____

_____

_____

_____

_____

_____

_____

_____

_____

_____

_____

December 28

What fears are you holding onto that are no longer serving you? How can you release these?

_____

_____

_____

_____

_____

_____

_____

_____

_____

_____

_____

_____

_____

December 29

Even if you can't change your situation today, if you do this one thing it will be a step in the right direction. That thing is...

_____

_____

_____

_____

_____

_____

_____

_____

_____

_____

_____

_____

December 30

What is one thing you can improve on (time management, communication, etc.), and how can you do this?

_____
_____
_____
_____
_____
_____
_____
_____
_____
_____
_____
_____
_____

December 31

What is your most cherished memory of this year?

_____

_____

_____

_____

_____

_____

_____

_____

_____

_____

_____

_____

_____

About the Author

Lisa McGrath is an international bestselling author, speaker, National Board Certified Teacher, and Achievement Coach. She has a private coaching practice committed to the personal excellence and empowerment of all people. Her vision is to personally impact the lives of a million people to live their best life, an Intentional Life, and to shift the paradigm around resignation, that is, that anyone can bring about positive change in their own lives and in the lives of others...if they believe they can. For information on personal coaching and courses, to request a speaking engagement, or to learn more about her books and programs, visit her website www.lisamcgrath.me or contact her at lisa@pageswithpurpose.com.

www.ingramcontent.com/pod-product-compliance
Lightning Source LLC
Chambersburg PA
CBHW061134120626
46546CB00005B/1785